Becoming Anchored Companion Journal

To

_____

From

_____

Becoming Anchored Companion Journal
Copyright © Thomas Bratton 2022

Published by Butterfly Books Publishing. Butterfly Books Publishing is an independent publisher.

Cover Design by C5 Designs
Interior Design by Butterfly Books Publishing

ISBN (print): 979-8-9859165-8-4

Printed in the United States of America

How to Use This Journal

If you don't yet have the *Becoming Anchored* devotional, get a copy here *amazon.com/dp/B0BL54MPVW*. Each week you're provided with a verse for reflection, some commentary, a question to consider, and space for prayer to implement into your life.

My hope is that you grow in hope, faith, and trust in God through this devotional and study. Use this Companion Journal each week as you go through the devotional to go deeper in your growth.

"For I know the plans I have for you," declares the Lord, "plans to prosper you and not to harm you, plans to give you hope and a future." Jeremiah 29:11. (NIV)

Letting Go

I choose to let go of these things:

_____

_____

_____

_____

_____

_____

_____

_____

Bless Forward

Who I can bless today or this week:

_____

_____

_____

_____

_____

_____

_____

Gratitude
What I'm grateful for.

_____

_____

_____

_____

_____

_____

_____

_____

_____

_____

_____

_____

_____

_____

_____

_____

_____

_____

_____

_____

Don't copy the customs and behaviors of this world, but let God transform you into a new person by changing the way you think. Then you will learn to know God's will for you, which is good and pleasing and perfect. Romans 12:2 (NLT)

Letting Go

I choose to let go of these things:

_____

_____

_____

_____

_____

_____

_____

_____

Bless Forward

Who I can bless today or this week:

_____

_____

_____

_____

_____

_____

_____

_____

Gratitude

What I'm grateful for.

_____

_____

_____

_____

_____

_____

_____

_____

_____

_____

_____

_____

_____

_____

_____

_____

_____

_____

_____

_____

For we are God's masterpiece. He has created us anew in Christ Jesus, so we can do the good things He planned for us a long time ago. Ephesians 2:10 (NLT)

Letting Go

I choose to let go of these things:

_____

_____

_____

_____

_____

_____

_____

_____

Bless Forward

Who I can bless today or this week:

_____

_____

_____

_____

_____

_____

_____

_____

Gratitude

What I'm grateful for.

_____

_____

_____

_____

_____

_____

_____

_____

_____

_____

_____

_____

_____

_____

_____

_____

_____

_____

_____

_____

_____

But those who hope in the Lord will renew their strength. They will soar on wings like eagles; they will run and not grow weary; they will walk and not be faint. Isaiah 40:31. (NIV)

Letting Go

I choose to let go of these things:

_____

_____

_____

_____

_____

_____

_____

_____

Bless Forward

Who I can bless today or this week:

_____

_____

_____

_____

_____

_____

_____

_____

Gratitude

What I'm grateful for.

_____

_____

_____

_____

_____

_____

_____

_____

_____

_____

_____

_____

_____

_____

_____

_____

_____

_____

_____

_____

See, I will do a new thing. It will begin happening now. Will you not know about it? I will even make a road in the wilderness, and rivers in the desert. Isaiah 43:19 (NLV)

Letting Go
I choose to let go of these things:

_____

_____

_____

_____

_____

_____

_____

Bless Forward
Who I can bless today or this week:

_____

_____

_____

_____

_____

_____

_____

Gratitude

What I'm grateful for:

_____

_____

_____

_____

_____

_____

_____

_____

_____

_____

_____

_____

_____

_____

_____

_____

_____

_____

_____

_____

_____

If I gave everything I have to the poor and even sacrificed my body, I could boast about it; but if I didn't love others, I would have gained nothing. 1 Corinthians 13:3 (NLT)

We should love one another. 1 John 3:11 (NLT)

Letting Go
I choose to let go of these things:

_____

_____

_____

_____

_____

_____

_____

_____

Bless Forward
Who I can bless today or this week:

_____

_____

_____

_____

_____

_____

_____

_____

Gratitude

What I'm grateful for.

_____

_____

_____

_____

_____

_____

_____

_____

_____

_____

_____

_____

_____

_____

_____

_____

_____

_____

Let's not merely say that we love each other; let us show the truth by our actions. 1 John 3:18 (NLT)

Letting Go
I choose to let go of these things:

_____

_____

_____

_____

_____

_____

_____

Bless Forward
Who I can bless today or this week:

_____

_____

_____

_____

_____

_____

_____

_____

Gratitude

What I'm grateful for.

_____

_____

_____

_____

_____

_____

_____

_____

_____

_____

_____

_____

_____

_____

_____

_____

_____

_____

_____

_____

For God loved the world so much that he gave his one and only Son, so that everyone who believes in him will not perish but have eternal life. John 3:16 (NLT)

Love is patient and kind. Love is not jealous or boastful or proud or rude. It does not demand its own way. It is not irritable, and it keeps no record of being wronged. 1 Corinthians 13:4-5 (NLT)

Letting Go

I choose to let go of these things:

_____

_____

_____

_____

_____

_____

_____

_____

Bless Forward

Who I can bless today or this week:

_____

_____

_____

_____

_____

_____

_____

_____

Gratitude

What I'm grateful for.

_____

_____

_____

_____

_____

_____

_____

_____

_____

_____

_____

_____

_____

_____

_____

_____

_____

_____

_____

*For God saved us and called us to live a **Holy** life. He did this, not because we deserved it, but because that was his plan from the beginning of time—to show us his grace through Christ Jesus. 2 Timothy 1:9 (NLT)*

Letting Go
I choose to let go of these things:

_____

_____

_____

_____

_____

_____

_____

Bless Forward
Who I can bless today or this week:

_____

_____

_____

_____

_____

_____

_____

_____

Gratitude

What I'm grateful for.

_____

_____

_____

_____

_____

_____

_____

_____

_____

_____

_____

_____

_____

_____

_____

_____

_____

_____

_____

_____

_____

But his wife said, "If the LORD were going to kill us, he wouldn't have accepted our burnt offering and grain offering. He wouldn't have appeared to us and told us this wonderful thing and done these miracles."
Judges 13:23 (NLT)

Letting Go
I choose to let go of these things:

_____

_____

_____

_____

_____

_____

_____

_____

Bless Forward
Who I can bless today or this week:

_____

_____

_____

_____

_____

_____

_____

_____

Gratitude

What I'm grateful for.

He renews my strength. He guides me along right paths, bringing honor to his name. Psalms 23:3 (NLT)

Letting Go
I choose to let go of these things:

_____

_____

_____

_____

_____

_____

_____

_____

Bless Forward
Who I can bless today or this week:

_____

_____

_____

_____

_____

_____

_____

_____

Gratitude

What I'm grateful for.

_____

_____

_____

_____

_____

_____

_____

_____

_____

_____

_____

_____

_____

_____

_____

_____

_____

_____

_____

_____

_____

_____

And I know it is important to love him with all my heart and all my understanding and all my strength, and to love my neighbor as myself. This is more important than to offer all of the burnt offerings and sacrifices required in the law. Mark 12:33 (NIV)

Letting Go

I choose to let go of these things:

_____

_____

_____

_____

_____

_____

_____

_____

Bless Forward

Who I can bless today or this week:

_____

_____

_____

_____

_____

_____

_____

_____

Gratitude

What I'm grateful for.

I am the good shepherd. The good shepherd sacrifices his life for the sheep. John 10:11 (NLT)

Letting Go
I choose to let go of these things:

_____

_____

_____

_____

_____

_____

_____

_____

Bless Forward
Who I can bless today or this week:

_____

_____

_____

_____

_____

_____

_____

_____

Gratitude

What I'm grateful for.

_____

_____

_____

_____

_____

_____

_____

_____

_____

_____

_____

_____

_____

_____

_____

_____

_____

_____

_____

_____

_____

_____

Don't worry about anything; instead, pray about everything. Tell God what you need and thank him for all he has done. Then you will experience God's peace, which exceeds anything we can understand. His peace will guard your hearts and minds as you live in Christ Jesus. Philippians 4:6-7 (NLT)

Letting Go

I choose to let go of these things:

_____

_____

_____

_____

_____

_____

_____

_____

Bless Forward

Who I can bless today or this week:

_____

_____

_____

_____

_____

_____

_____

_____

Gratitude

What I'm grateful for.

_____

_____

_____

_____

_____

_____

_____

_____

_____

_____

_____

_____

_____

_____

_____

_____

_____

_____

Neither our fears for today nor our worries about tomorrow—not even the powers of hell can separate us from God's love. Romans 8:38 (NLT)

Letting Go

I choose to let go of these things:

_____

_____

_____

_____

_____

_____

_____

Bless Forward

Who I can bless today or this week:

_____

_____

_____

_____

_____

_____

_____

Gratitude

What I'm grateful for.

_____

_____

_____

_____

_____

_____

_____

_____

_____

_____

_____

_____

_____

_____

_____

_____

_____

_____

_____

_____

_____

Letting Go

I choose to let go of these things:

_____

_____

_____

_____

_____

_____

_____

_____

Bless Forward

Who I can bless today or this week:

_____

_____

_____

_____

_____

_____

_____

_____

Gratitude

What I'm grateful for.

_____

_____

_____

_____

_____

_____

_____

_____

_____

_____

_____

_____

_____

_____

_____

_____

_____

_____

_____

_____

_____

For by grace, you have been saved through faith, and that not of yourselves; it is the gift of God, not of works, lest anyone should boast. Ephesians 2:8-9 (NKJV)

Letting Go
I choose to let go of these things:

_____

_____

_____

_____

_____

_____

_____

Bless Forward
Who I can bless today or this week:

_____

_____

_____

_____

_____

_____

_____

_____

Gratitude

What I'm grateful for.

_____

_____

_____

_____

_____

_____

_____

_____

_____

_____

_____

_____

_____

_____

_____

_____

_____

_____

_____

_____

_____

_____

_____

Therefore, as God's chosen people, holy and dearly loved, clothe yourselves with compassion, kindness, humility, gentleness, and patience. Colossians 3:12 (NIV)

Letting Go
I choose to let go of these things:

_____

_____

_____

_____

_____

_____

_____

_____

Bless Forward
Who I can bless today or this week:

_____

_____

_____

_____

_____

_____

_____

_____

Gratitude

What I'm grateful for.

_____

_____

_____

_____

_____

_____

_____

_____

_____

_____

_____

_____

_____

_____

_____

_____

_____

_____

_____

But because of his great love for us, God, who is rich in mercy, made us alive with Christ even when we were dead in transgressions—it is by grace you have been saved. Ephesians 2:4-5 (NIV)

Letting Go
I choose to let go of these things:

_____

_____

_____

_____

_____

_____

_____

Bless Forward
Who I can bless today or this week:

_____

_____

_____

_____

_____

_____

_____

_____

Gratitude

What I'm grateful for.

_____

_____

_____

_____

_____

_____

_____

_____

_____

_____

_____

_____

_____

_____

_____

_____

_____

_____

_____

_____

As you know, we count as blessed those who have persevered. You have heard of Job's perseverance and have seen what the Lord finally brought about. The Lord is full of compassion and mercy. James 5:11 (NIV)

Letting Go
I choose to let go of these things:

_____

_____

_____

_____

_____

_____

_____

Bless Forward
Who I can bless today or this week:

_____

_____

_____

_____

_____

_____

_____

_____

Gratitude

What I'm grateful for.

_____

_____

_____

_____

_____

_____

_____

_____

_____

_____

_____

_____

_____

_____

_____

_____

_____

_____

_____

_____

_____

_____

So, let's not get tired of doing what is good. At just the right time we will reap a harvest of blessing if we don't give up. Galatians 6:9. (NLT)

Letting Go
I choose to let go of these things:

_____

_____

_____

_____

_____

_____

_____

_____

Bless Forward
Who I can bless today or this week:

_____

_____

_____

_____

_____

_____

_____

_____

Gratitude

What I'm grateful for:

If you remain in me and my words remain in you, you may ask for anything you want, and it will be granted! John 15:7. (NLT)

Letting Go

I choose to let go of these things:

_____

_____

_____

_____

_____

_____

_____

Bless Forward

Who I can bless today or this week:

_____

_____

_____

_____

_____

_____

_____

Gratitude

What I'm grateful for.

_____

_____

_____

_____

_____

_____

_____

_____

_____

_____

_____

_____

_____

_____

_____

_____

_____

_____

_____

"Keep on asking, and you will receive what you ask for. Keep on seeking, and you will find. Keep on knocking, and the door will be opened to you. For everyone who asks, receives. Everyone who seeks, finds. And to everyone who knocks, the door will be opened." Luke 7: 7-8 (NLT)

Letting Go

I choose to let go of these things:

_____

_____

_____

_____

_____

_____

_____

Bless Forward

Who I can bless today or this week:

_____

_____

_____

_____

_____

_____

_____

_____

Gratitude

What I'm grateful for.

_____

_____

_____

_____

_____

_____

_____

_____

_____

_____

_____

_____

_____

_____

_____

_____

_____

_____

_____

_____

_____

_____

For God presented Jesus as the sacrifice for sin. People are made right with God when they believe that Jesus sacrificed his life, shedding his blood. This sacrifice shows that God was being fair when he held back and did not punish those who sinned in times past. Romans 3:25 (NLT)

Letting Go

I choose to let go of these things:

_____

_____

_____

_____

_____

_____

_____

_____

Bless Forward

Who I can bless today or this week:

_____

_____

_____

_____

_____

_____

_____

_____

Gratitude

What I'm grateful for.

_____

_____

_____

_____

_____

_____

_____

_____

_____

_____

_____

_____

_____

_____

_____

_____

_____

_____

_____

_____

Forget the former things; do not dwell on the past. Isaiah 43:18 (NIV)

Letting Go

I choose to let go of these things:

_____

_____

_____

_____

_____

_____

_____

_____

Bless Forward

Who I can bless today or this week:

_____

_____

_____

_____

_____

_____

_____

_____

Gratitude

What I'm grateful for.

_____

_____

_____

_____

_____

_____

_____

_____

_____

_____

_____

_____

_____

_____

_____

_____

_____

_____

_____

_____

_____

_____

I don't mean to say that I have already achieved these things or that I have already reached perfection. But I press on to possess that perfection for which Christ Jesus first possessed me. No, dear brothers and sisters, I have not achieved it, but I focus on this one thing: Forgetting the past and looking forward to what lies ahead, I press on to reach the end of the race and receive the heavenly prize for which God, through Christ Jesus, is calling us. Philippians 3:12-14 (NLT)

Letting Go

I choose to let go of these things:

_____

_____

_____

_____

_____

_____

_____

_____

Bless Forward

Who I can bless today or this week:

_____

_____

_____

_____

_____

_____

_____

_____

Gratitude

What I'm grateful for.

_____

_____

_____

_____

_____

_____

_____

_____

_____

_____

_____

_____

_____

_____

_____

_____

_____

_____

_____

So do not worry about tomorrow. Tomorrow will have its own worries. Today's trouble is enough for today.
Matthew 6:34 (NLT)

Letting Go

I choose to let go of these things:

_____

_____

_____

_____

_____

_____

_____

Bless Forward

Who I can bless today or this week:

_____

_____

_____

_____

_____

_____

_____

Gratitude

What I'm grateful for.

_____

_____

_____

_____

_____

_____

_____

_____

_____

_____

_____

_____

_____

_____

_____

_____

_____

_____

_____

_____

Seek the Kingdom of God above all else, and live righteously, and he will give you everything you need.
Matthew 6:33 (NLT)

Letting Go

I choose to let go of these things:

_____

_____

_____

_____

_____

_____

_____

Bless Forward

Who I can bless today or this week:

_____

_____

_____

_____

_____

_____

_____

Gratitude

What I'm grateful for.

_____

_____

_____

_____

_____

_____

_____

_____

_____

_____

_____

_____

_____

_____

_____

_____

_____

_____

Trust in the Lord with all your heart and lean not on your own understanding; in all ways submit to Him, and He will make your paths straight. Proverbs 3:5-6 (NIV)

Letting Go

I choose to let go of these things:

_____

_____

_____

_____

_____

_____

_____

Bless Forward

Who I can bless today or this week:

_____

_____

_____

_____

_____

_____

_____

Gratitude

What I'm grateful for.

_____

_____

_____

_____

_____

_____

_____

_____

_____

_____

_____

_____

_____

_____

_____

_____

_____

_____

_____

_____

Love never gives up, never loses faith, is always hopeful, and endures through every circumstance.
1 Corinthians 13:7 (NLT)

Letting Go
I choose to let go of these things:

_____

_____

_____

_____

_____

_____

_____

Bless Forward
Who I can bless today or this week:

_____

_____

_____

_____

_____

_____

_____

Gratitude

What I'm grateful for.

_____

_____

_____

_____

_____

_____

_____

_____

_____

_____

_____

_____

_____

_____

_____

_____

_____

_____

_____

And we know that in all things God works for the good of those who love him, who have been called according to his purpose. Romans 8:28 (NIV)

Letting Go

I choose to let go of these things:

_____

_____

_____

_____

_____

_____

_____

_____

Bless Forward

Who I can bless today or this week:

_____

_____

_____

_____

_____

_____

_____

_____

Gratitude

What I'm grateful for.

_____

_____

_____

_____

_____

_____

_____

_____

_____

_____

_____

_____

_____

_____

_____

_____

_____

_____

_____

_____

_____

Fix your thoughts on what is true, and honorable, and right, and pure, and lovely, and admirable. Think about things that are excellent and worthy of praise. Philippians 4:8 9 (NLT)

Letting Go
I choose to let go of these things:

_____

_____

_____

_____

_____

_____

_____

Bless Forward
Who I can bless today or this week:

_____

_____

_____

_____

_____

_____

_____

Gratitude

What I'm grateful for.

_____

_____

_____

_____

_____

_____

_____

_____

_____

_____

_____

_____

_____

_____

_____

_____

_____

_____

_____

With man this is impossible, but with God all things are possible. Matthew 19:26 (NIV)

Letting Go

I choose to let go of these things:

_____

_____

_____

_____

_____

_____

_____

_____

Bless Forward

Who I can bless today or this week:

_____

_____

_____

_____

_____

_____

_____

_____

Gratitude

What I'm grateful for.

_____

_____

_____

_____

_____

_____

_____

_____

_____

_____

_____

_____

_____

_____

_____

_____

_____

_____

_____

_____

_____

This is the Day that the Lord has made. Let us be full of joy and be glad in it. Psalms 118:24 (NLV)

Letting Go
I choose to let go of these things:

_____

_____

_____

_____

_____

_____

_____

_____

Bless Forward
Who I can bless today or this week:

_____

_____

_____

_____

_____

_____

_____

_____

Gratitude

What I'm grateful for.

"Come to me, all of you who are weary and carry heavy burdens, and I will give you rest."
Matthew 11:28 (NIV)

Letting Go
I choose to let go of these things:

_____

_____

_____

_____

_____

_____

_____

_____

Bless Forward
Who I can bless today or this week:

_____

_____

_____

_____

_____

_____

_____

_____

Gratitude

What I'm grateful for:

_____

_____

_____

_____

_____

_____

_____

_____

_____

_____

_____

_____

_____

_____

_____

_____

_____

_____

_____

_____

_____

We have been beaten, been put in prison, faced angry mobs, worked to exhaustion, endured sleepless nights, and gone without food. 2 Corinthians 6:5 (NLT)

Letting Go
I choose to let go of these things:

_____

_____

_____

_____

_____

_____

_____

_____

Bless Forward
Who I can bless today or this week:

_____

_____

_____

_____

_____

_____

_____

_____

Gratitude

What I'm grateful for.

Jesus went to the grave with a sad heart. The grave was a hole on the side of a hill. A stone covered the door. "Roll the stone aside," Jesus told them. John 11:38-39 (NLV)

Letting Go
I choose to let go of these things:

_____

_____

_____

_____

_____

_____

_____

_____

Bless Forward
Who I can bless today or this week:

_____

_____

_____

_____

_____

_____

_____

_____

Gratitude

What I'm grateful for.

_____

_____

_____

_____

_____

_____

_____

_____

_____

_____

_____

_____

_____

_____

_____

_____

_____

_____

_____

_____

Be strong and courageous. Do not be afraid; do not be discouraged, for the LORD your God will be with you wherever you go. Joshua 1:9 (NLT)

Letting Go
I choose to let go of these things:

_____

_____

_____

_____

_____

_____

_____

Bless Forward
Who I can bless today or this week:

_____

_____

_____

_____

_____

_____

_____

Gratitude

What I'm grateful for.

_____

_____

_____

_____

_____

_____

_____

_____

_____

_____

_____

_____

_____

_____

_____

_____

_____

_____

_____

_____

Shouldn't you have mercy on your fellow servant, just as I had mercy on you? That's what my heavenly Father will do to you if you refuse to forgive your brothers and sisters from your heart. Matthew 18:33,35 (NIV)

Letting Go

I choose to let go of these things:

_____

_____

_____

_____

_____

_____

_____

_____

Bless Forward

Who I can bless today or this week:

_____

_____

_____

_____

_____

_____

_____

_____

Gratitude

What I'm grateful for.

_____

_____

_____

_____

_____

_____

_____

_____

_____

_____

_____

_____

_____

_____

_____

_____

_____

_____

_____

_____

When troubles come your way, consider it an opportunity for great joy. James 1:2 (NIV)

Letting Go

I choose to let go of these things:

_____

_____

_____

_____

_____

_____

_____

Bless Forward

Who I can bless today or this week:

_____

_____

_____

_____

_____

_____

_____

Gratitude

What I'm grateful for.

Don't be afraid, for I am with you. Don't be discouraged, for I am your God. I will strengthen you and help you. I will hold you up with my victorious right hand. Isaiah 41:10 (NLT)

Letting Go

I choose to let go of these things:

_____

_____

_____

_____

_____

_____

_____

_____

Bless Forward

Who I can bless today or this week:

_____

_____

_____

_____

_____

_____

_____

_____

Gratitude

What I'm grateful for:

_____

_____

_____

_____

_____

_____

_____

_____

_____

_____

_____

_____

_____

_____

_____

_____

_____

_____

_____

_____

_____

_____

We believe it is through the grace of our Lord Jesus that we are saved, just as they are. Acts 15:11 (NIV)

Letting Go
I choose to let go of these things:

_____

_____

_____

_____

_____

_____

_____

Bless Forward
Who I can bless today or this week:

_____

_____

_____

_____

_____

_____

_____

Gratitude

What I'm grateful for.

_____

_____

_____

_____

_____

_____

_____

_____

_____

_____

_____

_____

_____

_____

_____

_____

_____

_____

_____

But as a mountain erodes and crumbles and as a rock is moved from its place, as water wears away stones and torrents wash away the soil, so you destroy a person's hope. Job 14:18-19 (NIV)

Letting Go
I choose to let go of these things:

_____

_____

_____

_____

_____

_____

_____

Bless Forward
Who I can bless today or this week:

_____

_____

_____

_____

_____

_____

_____

_____

Gratitude

What I'm grateful for.

Our great desire is that you will keep on loving others as long as life lasts, in order to make certain that what you hope for will come true. Hebrews 6:11 (NLT)

Letting Go

I choose to let go of these things:

_____

_____

_____

_____

_____

_____

_____

Bless Forward

Who I can bless today or this week:

_____

_____

_____

_____

_____

_____

_____

Gratitude

What I'm grateful for.

_____

_____

_____

_____

_____

_____

_____

_____

_____

_____

_____

_____

_____

_____

_____

_____

_____

_____

Blessed is the one who perseveres under trial because, having stood the test, that person will receive the crown of life that the Lord has promised to those who love him. James 1:12 (NIV)

Letting Go
I choose to let go of these things:

_____

_____

_____

_____

_____

_____

_____

Bless Forward
Who I can bless today or this week:

_____

_____

_____

_____

_____

_____

_____

_____

Gratitude

What I'm grateful for.

_____

_____

_____

_____

_____

_____

_____

_____

_____

_____

_____

_____

_____

_____

_____

_____

_____

_____

You are my refuge and my shield; your word is my source of hope. Psalms 119:114 (NLT)

Letting Go
I choose to let go of these things:

_____

_____

_____

_____

_____

_____

_____

_____

Bless Forward
Who I can bless today or this week:

_____

_____

_____

_____

_____

_____

_____

_____

Gratitude

What I'm grateful for.

_____

_____

_____

_____

_____

_____

_____

_____

_____

_____

_____

_____

_____

_____

_____

_____

_____

_____

_____

Jesus said to His followers, "Because of this, I say to you, do not worry about your life, what you are going to eat. Do not worry about your body, what you are going to wear." Luke 12:22 (NLV)

Letting Go
I choose to let go of these things:

_____

_____

_____

_____

_____

_____

_____

_____

Bless Forward
Who I can bless today or this week:

_____

_____

_____

_____

_____

_____

_____

_____

Gratitude

What I'm grateful for.

_____

_____

_____

_____

_____

_____

_____

_____

_____

_____

_____

_____

_____

_____

_____

_____

_____

_____

_____

_____

_____

_____

Letting Go
I choose to let go of these things:

_____

_____

_____

_____

_____

_____

_____

Bless Forward
Who I can bless today or this week:

_____

_____

_____

_____

_____

_____

_____

_____

Gratitude

What I'm grateful for.

_____

_____

_____

_____

_____

_____

_____

_____

_____

_____

_____

_____

_____

_____

_____

_____

_____

_____

_____

_____

Delight yourself also in the Lord, and He shall give you the desires of your heart. Psalm 37:4 (NIV)

Letting Go
I choose to let go of these things:

_____

_____

_____

_____

_____

_____

_____

Bless Forward
Who I can bless today or this week:

_____

_____

_____

_____

_____

_____

_____

Gratitude

What I'm grateful for.

Letting Go

I choose to let go of these things:

Bless Forward

Who I can bless today or this week:

Gratitude

What I'm grateful for.

_____

_____

_____

_____

_____

_____

_____

_____

_____

_____

_____

_____

_____

_____

_____

_____

_____

_____

_____

_____

_____

_____

Rejoice in our confident hope, be patient in trouble, and keep on praying. Romans 12:12 (NLV)

Letting Go

I choose to let go of these things:

_____

_____

_____

_____

_____

_____

_____

_____

Bless Forward

Who I can bless today or this week:

_____

_____

_____

_____

_____

_____

_____

_____

_____

Gratitude

What I'm grateful for.

_____

_____

_____

_____

_____

_____

_____

_____

_____

_____

_____

_____

_____

_____

_____

_____

_____

_____

_____

And we know God causes everything to work together for the good of those who Love God and are called according to His purpose. Romans 8:28 (NIV)

Letting Go
I choose to let go of these things:

_____

_____

_____

_____

_____

_____

_____

_____

Bless Forward
Who I can bless today or this week:

_____

_____

_____

_____

_____

_____

_____

_____

Gratitude

What I'm grateful for.

_____

_____

_____

_____

_____

_____

_____

_____

_____

_____

_____

_____

_____

_____

_____

_____

_____

_____

_____

_____

_____